Did Jesus Wear Blue Jeans?

Answers to a child's first Bible questions

By Betsy Rosen Elliot • Illustrated by Don Page

What is a Gospel?

What is a Gospel?

Gospel means *good news* in Greek. The Gospels are the first four books of the New Testament. They tell about Jesus and how he came to earth to show us God's love by his life, death and rising to life again. He gave us a new start with God. That's certainly good news!

Why do we have four Gospels?

The four Gospels were written for four different reasons. Matthew wrote his Gosp[el] for Jewish people. Mark wrote his to give t[he] basic facts (it is the shortest). Luke wrote [his] Gospel to give all the details of Jesus' life. John wrote his Gospel to show that Jesus i[s] our Savior, or rescuer.

Who wrote the New Testament?

There are 27 books in the New Testament and many people wrote them! Jesus' friends wrote some. Paul, who once hated Christians and later became a Christian himself, wrote many others. Luke was a doctor and he wrote a Gospel and the book of Acts.

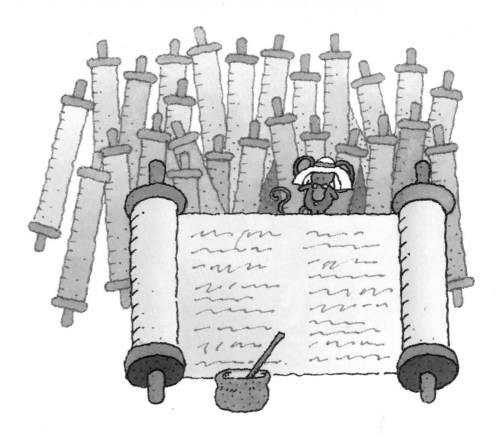

YOUR MAIL, MADAM.

Are the New Testament letters like the ones we write today?

Yes, except they weren't written on paper and envelopes and mailed. They were usually written on rolled-up scrolls made of parchment, and they were carried by messengers or travelers. Some of the letters were written to one person, but most were sent to churches and read to everyone.

Why was Jesus born in a stable?

Why was Jesus born in a stable?
All the inns in Bethlehem were full and Mary and Joseph needed a place to stay. Since there were no rooms, Mary and Joseph stayed in a stable and that's where Jesus was born. Jesus actually slept in a manger. A manger is the box that holds clean hay for the animals.

Why did the three wise men bring such strange gifts?
God was showing the three wise men who Jesus would grow up to be. Gold showed Jesus would become a king. Frankincense showed that Jesus should be worshiped. Myrrh showed that Jesus' death was to be very important.

What was Jesus' last name?

Jesus didn't have a last name. People in Jesus' time were often given their name by where they lived, such as *Saul of Tarsus*, or by their fathers, like *James and John, sons of Zebedee*. When we say *Jesus Christ*, the word *Christ* isn't his last name. It means that Jesus was the Christ, or Savior. People also called him *Jesus of Nazareth*.

Was Jesus ever naughty?

Jesus was a person just like you and me, but he never, ever did anything wrong! His parents did get cross with him though. When he was 12 years old, he was traveling with his parents and they lost him. They were with a large group so they didn't realize at first that he was missing. They found him in the temple, asking and answering questions.

Did Jesus wear blue jeans?

Did Jesus wear blue jeans?
Jesus didn't wear blue jeans; they weren't invented back then. In fact, men didn't wear pants until hundreds of years later. Because Jesus lived in a hot country, he wore light-colored, loose-fitting robes.

What did the 12 disciples do before they met Jesus?
The 12 men who became Jesus' closest followers had different kinds of jobs. Peter, Andrew, James, and John were fishermen. Matthew was a tax collector. Simon might have been a political leader.

Who were some of Jesus' closest friends?

Peter, James, and John seemed to be Jesus' closest friends. One day Jesus took them on a mountain top to show them what a special messenger of God he was. And as he died, Jesus told his mother and John to be like mother and son.

Why was Peter nicknamed *Rock*?

The name *Peter* in Greek is *Petros*. This means *rock*. So Jesus was saying that Peter could be as solid as a rock. Peter lived up to his nickname. He became a great leader in the early church.

Did Jesus know Moses?

Did Jesus know Moses?
No, Jesus didn't know Moses because Jesus was born more than 1,000 years later. But Jesus knew a lot about Moses. Also, Moses appeared with Jesus on a mountain top. This showed Jesus' friends how special Jesus was.

Why did the paralyzed man go through the roof?
A man who couldn't walk had some clever friends. They couldn't get through the door of the house where Jesus was because of all the people. So they removed part of the roof! They lowered the man down on ropes so that Jesus could heal him!

Why did Zacchaeus climb a tree?
Zacchaeus was a short man and he couldn't see Jesus over the crowd. So he climbed a tree to get a better view. Jesus noticed Zacchaeus and invited himself to Zacchaeus' house. Zacchaeus became a loyal follower of Jesus that day.

Who washed Jesus' feet?

Jesus was at a special dinner the week before he died. Mary, who was the sister of Lazarus and Martha, poured expensive perfume on Jesus' feet and gently washed them. Instead of using a towel, she dried Jesus' feet with her hair. Some people criticized Mary, but Jesus said she'd done a wonderful thing.

Did Jesus like children?

Children were special to Jesus. One time, Jesus' friends made some children go away. They thought the children were bothering Jesus. But Jesus told the children to stay; he said grown-ups could learn a lot from children!

What is a miracle?

What is a miracle?

A miracle is a wonderful thing that only God can do. Jesus did many miracles to help and heal people. It was a miracle when Jesus told the fierce storm to stop, and it did! These miracles proved that Jesus was God as well as man.

What was the first miracle Jesus did?

Jesus and his friends went to a wedding. Jesus' mother was there too. At the wedding party, the wine suddenly ran out. Jesus asked for some big jars to be filled with water and he turned the water into wine!

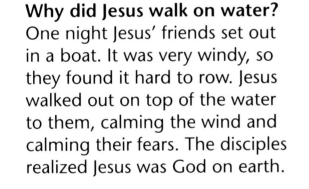

What other miracles did Jesus do?

Jesus brought some dead people back to life. He healed many who couldn't walk. He put mud on a blind man's eyes to make him see! He touched a man's tongue to make him talk! Twice Jesus fed thousands of people with just a little bit of food.

Why did Jesus walk on water?

One night Jesus' friends set out in a boat. It was very windy, so they found it hard to row. Jesus walked out on top of the water to them, calming the wind and calming their fears. The disciples realized Jesus was God on earth.

Did Jesus tell jokes?

Did Jesus tell jokes?

Jesus enjoyed life, and he could see the funny side of things. He seemed to like word jokes a lot. Once he said some people avoid little sins but ignore big ones. He said it is like someone who strains out a tiny bug from their drinking water ... but doesn't notice the camel in it!

Who got a job feeding pigs?

Jesus told a story about a man who left home to spend his money on silly things. Soon his money ran out and he had to feed pigs. He went back home and told his father he was sorry. His father welcomed him and gave him a big hug. That's just like God welcomes us when we are sorry.

Why did Jesus say people were like sheep?

Jesus said people were like sheep because sheep are not the smartest animals! Sheep need protection from enemies such as wolves or bears. They need a shepherd to care for them. Like sheep, people can easily follow wrong ways too. That's why we can be glad that Jesus is our Good Shepherd.

Jesus was God, so why did he pray?

Jesus was God the Son on earth, but he was also a real human being. So Jesus prayed for the same reasons we do: to thank God, to worship, to ask for help for himself and for others.

Why did Jesus ride a donkey?

Why did Jesus ride a donkey?
Jesus rode a gentle donkey into Jerusalem on Palm Sunday. He could have ridden a mighty war-horse, but he wanted to show that he was bringing peace and love.

What was the *last supper*?
The *last supper* was the last meal that Jesus and his disciples ate together. It was a Passover meal, a special supper to remember when the Israelites left Egypt. It was also special because it was the first Communion, a new way Jesus gave to remember him.

Why didn't Jesus defend himself?
Jesus was certainly powerful enough to fight back when he was arrested and nailed on the cross. But he knew that it was God's plan for him to die so that all people could have new life.

Why did Jesus wash his friends' feet?
When Jesus took a bowl of water and a towel and knelt to wash their feet, his friends were very surprised! This was the job of the least important servant, and Jesus was their master! Jesus wanted to show them he loved them and that they should serve one another.

Why did the sky turn dark?
When Jesus died, the sky turned dark for three hours. It was a sign from God that the most important event of history had happened.

Who rolled the stone away?

Who rolled the stone away?
Jesus was buried in a tomb like a cave
with a huge stone in front to block the
entrance. There were guards around the
tomb to stop anyone from stealing Jesus'
body. Matthew's Gospel says that an
angel rolled the stone away.

Why did Jesus come back from the dead?
Jesus came back from the dead to prove he was
more powerful even than death. He was God
as well as a man, so death could not beat him.
Jesus wanted to show his disciples (and us!) that
he was worth believing in. He also had some
work for them (and us!) to do here on earth; to
share the good news.

Where is Jesus now?
Jesus is in Heaven now, preparing a place for us. He has given us his own spirit, the Holy Spirit, to help us each day.

What will happen when Jesus comes back?
The Bible tells us that a new Heaven and a new earth will begin when Jesus comes back to earth.

What was the first church like?

What was the first church like?
The first Christians didn't meet in church buildings. They met in homes because it was illegal and even dangerous to meet. But they met together for the same reasons we do: to worship God, to learn about Jesus, to pray, and to be with believers.

SHHH....

Were God's people always called Christians?
After Jesus died Christians were called *believers* or *followers of the Way*. Later the word *Christian* was used. It means *belonging to Christ*. When it was dangerous to be known as a Christian, Christians had a secret sign. The secret sign of a Christian was the sign of the fish.

What happened to the 12 disciples?

Some of the disciples, like Peter and John, became important leaders in the church. Some were killed for believing in Jesus. Some wrote books in the New Testament. John's pen was busy: he wrote a Gospel, three letters, and the book of Revelation!

Where did Paul go on his travels?

Paul traveled in Europe, especially in Greece, and in Asia sharing the good news of Jesus. He traveled by boat and on land and he even got shipwrecked. On different trips Barnabas, John Mark, and Luke went with him.

Why was Paul in prison?

Paul was put in prison at least five times! He was being punished for telling the good news about Jesus. Some people were afraid of the power of this message. They thought that by stopping the messenger, they could stop the message. But they were wrong! Churches just kept growing and the good news just kept spreading.